Be a BUG DETECTIVE

Written by
Andy Charman and **Sarah Erskine**
Illustrated by
David Anstey

CONTENTS

Derrydale Books
New York

What is an insect?

There are insects almost everywhere you go. They live in the soil, on plants, in rivers, lakes, and ponds, and in dark caves – everywhere from dry deserts to the snowy peaks of mountaintops.

Insects are the largest group of creatures in the natural world. For every person living on this planet there are about 200 million insects. Over a million different kinds, or ***species****, are known and there may be many more.*

Insects have a bad name because some of them cause diseases and damage our crops. Luckily, only a small number are harmful to us. In fact, insects are vital to life on earth.

Beetles There are over 30,000 different kinds of beetle. Their forewings have developed into hard wing cases that protect the body and delicate hind wings.

Bees Of the 19,000 known species of bee most are solitary, that is, they live on their own. Bumble bees and honey bees are unusual because they live in large colonies.

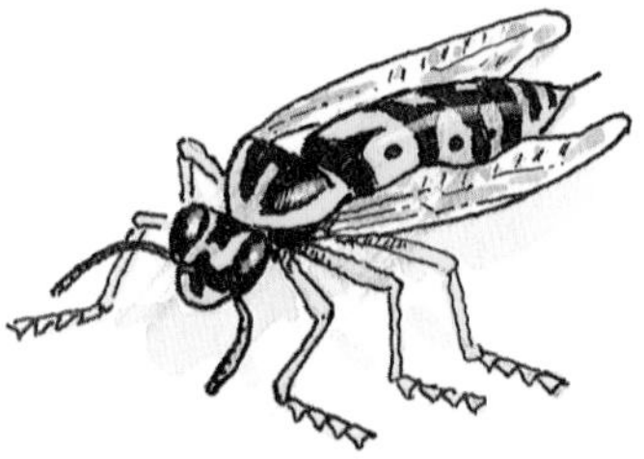

Wasps There are 20,000 different kinds of wasp. Some live alone, others live in large groups, or *colonies*. Many kinds of wasps build nests of paper that they make by chewing up wood and mixing it with saliva.

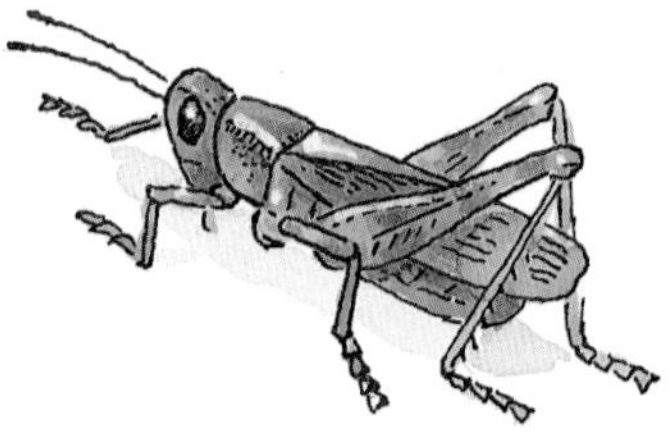

Crickets and grasshoppers These insects have long back legs made for jumping. Most kinds live on plant stems and leaves, and grasses.

Ants There are 8,000 different kinds of ant, all of which live in colonies. They vary in size but all ants have a narrow "waist" between the thorax and abdomen.

Bugs The title of this book uses the word "bug" to mean all kinds of insects. But there is a group of insects called bugs. The largest bugs have wings that are hard at the base and soft at the tip.

The naming of parts

Insects are *invertebrates*, which means that they do not have a backbone to support their bodies. Instead, they have a hard outer skin, or *cuticle*. An insect's body is divided into three parts: the *head*, *thorax*, and *abdomen*. The insect's eyes and mouthparts are on its head. The mouthparts differ according to the kind of food the insect eats.

The insect's legs and wings are on the thorax. All insects have three pairs of legs, and one or two pairs of wings. The abdomen carries the parts of the body that are to do with breaking down food, producing young, and getting rid of waste.

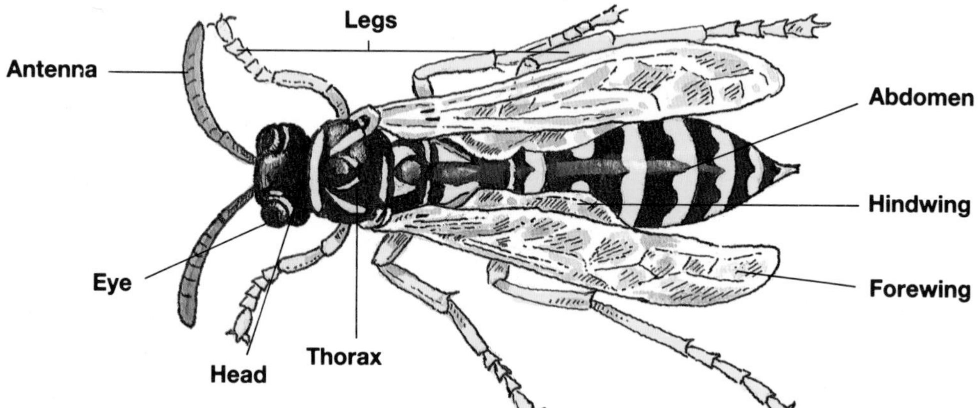

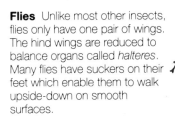

Flies Unlike most other insects, flies only have one pair of wings. The hind wings are reduced to balance organs called *halteres*. Many flies have suckers on their feet which enable them to walk upside-down on smooth surfaces.

Dragonflies and damselflies These two kinds of insects are fast fliers and have good eyesight. They catch flies in the air and eat them with their powerful jaws.

Butterflies and moths The bodies and wings of these insects are covered in tiny scales which give them their beautiful colors. Most butterflies have *antennae* which end in a tiny club; moths do not.

Cockroaches These insects are found almost everywhere and they eat just about anything. Many kinds live in buildings. They hide in narrow crevices and come out at night to feed on scraps of food.

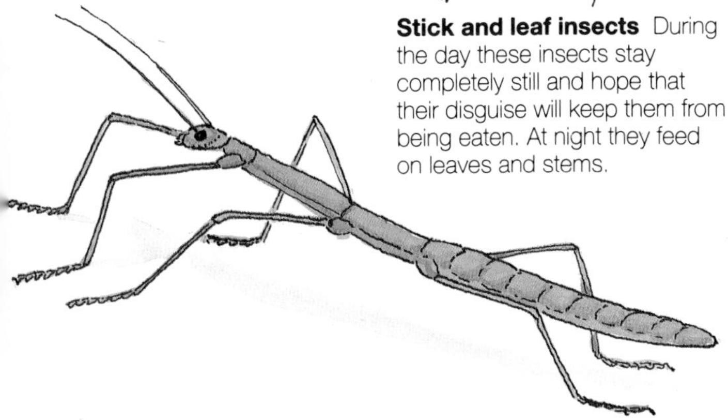

Stick and leaf insects During the day these insects stay completely still and hope that their disguise will keep them from being eaten. At night they feed on leaves and stems.

Spot the insect

Here is a collection of "creepy-crawlies," some of which you may have met in real life. Not all of them are insects. Remember what you've read about insects so far and pick out the ones that fit the description.

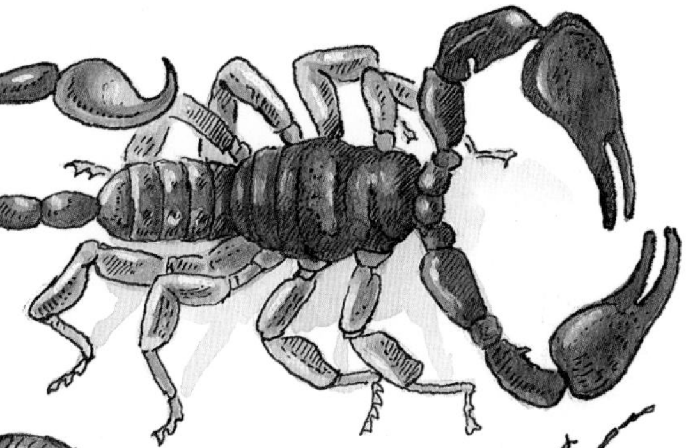

1.

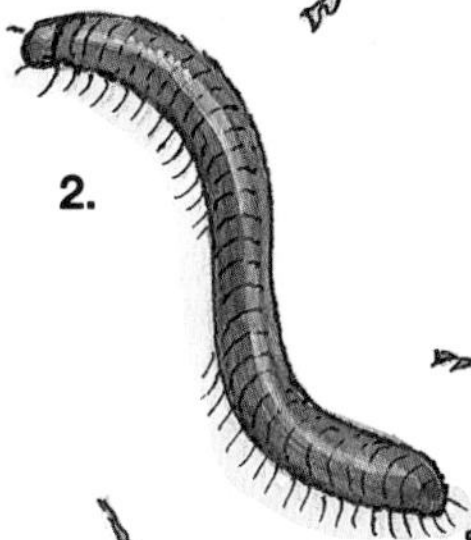

2.

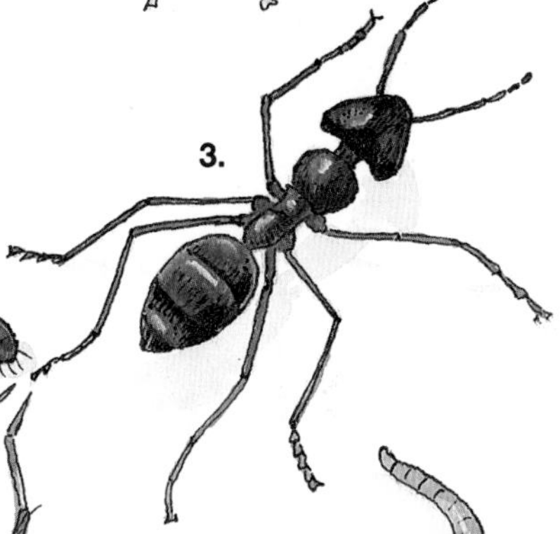

3.

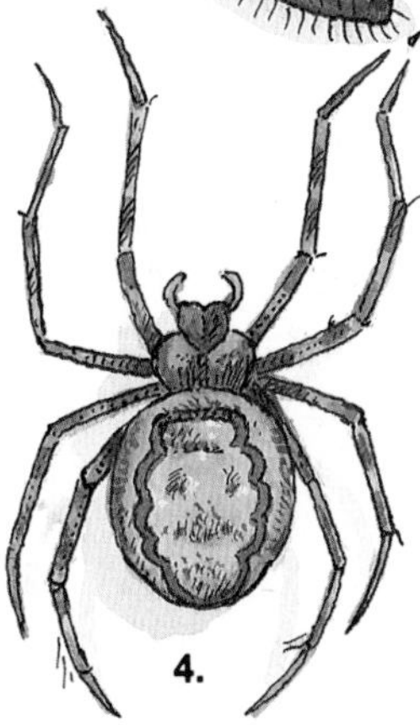

4.

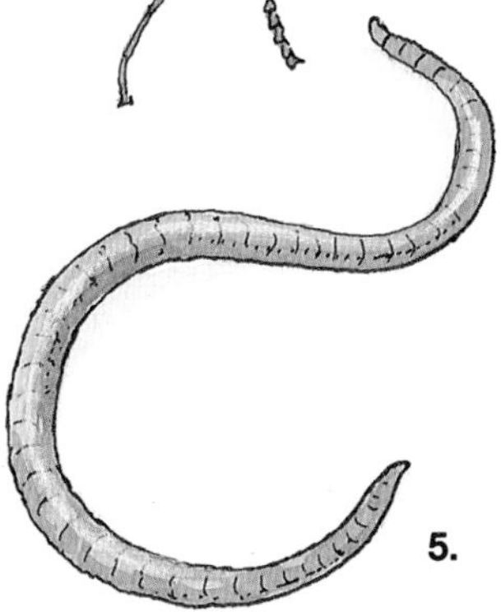

5.

ANSWERS

SPOT THE INSECT

1. is a **scorpion** and not an insect. It has four pairs of legs and two body sections.

2. is a **centipede** and not an insect. It has a huge number of legs and its body is in many sections.

3. is an **ant.** It is an insect. It has antennae, three pairs of legs, and three body sections.

4. is a **spider** and not an insect. It has four pairs of legs.

5. is an **earthworm.** It has no legs and its body is not divided into three sections.

Life cycles

Most insects start life as eggs. These hatch into ***larvae*** *and become adults by either complete or incomplete* ***metamorphosis****. Bees, butterflies, beetles, and flies are examples of insects that undergo complete metamorphosis. This kind of life cycle enables the larvae and adults to live very different lives. The larvae are the feeding and growing stages. The adults spend most of their time and energy looking for mates and finding new places to lay their eggs. Some adult insects, such as butterflies, eat energy-rich* ***nectar****.*

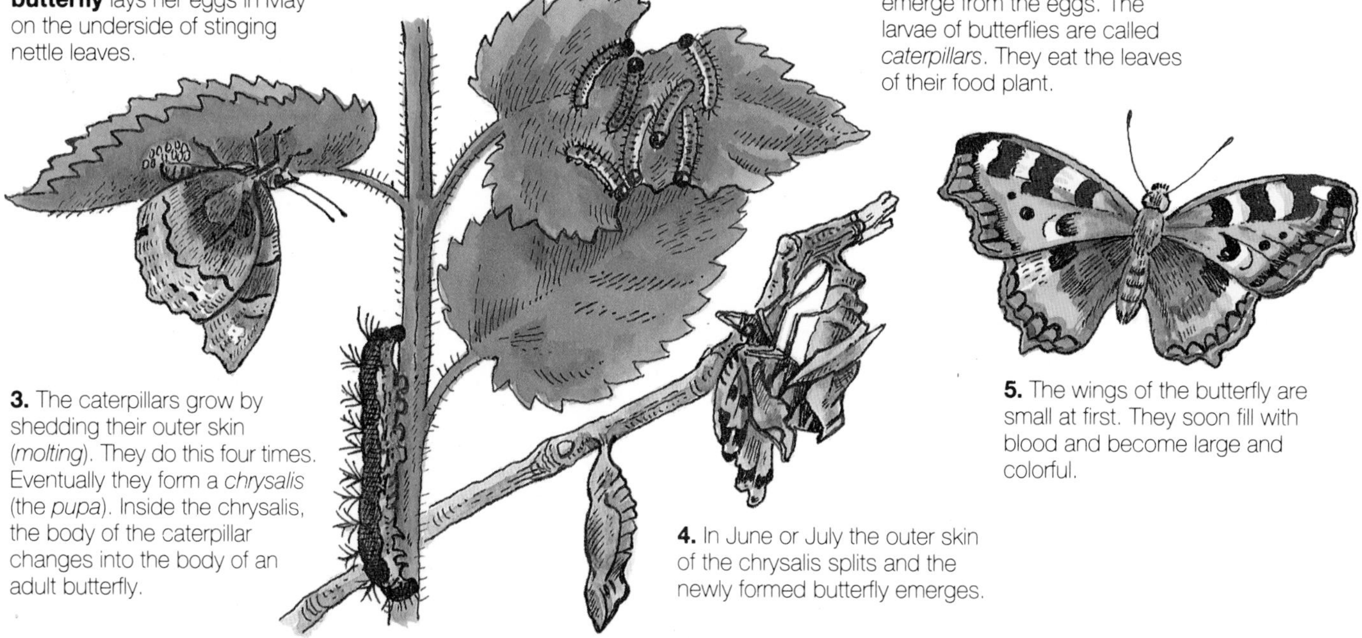

1. The female **tortoiseshell butterfly** lays her eggs in May on the underside of stinging nettle leaves.

2. After two weeks, the larvae emerge from the eggs. The larvae of butterflies are called *caterpillars*. They eat the leaves of their food plant.

3. The caterpillars grow by shedding their outer skin (*molting*). They do this four times. Eventually they form a *chrysalis* (the *pupa*). Inside the chrysalis, the body of the caterpillar changes into the body of an adult butterfly.

4. In June or July the outer skin of the chrysalis splits and the newly formed butterfly emerges.

5. The wings of the butterfly are small at first. They soon fill with blood and become large and colorful.

ALL CHANGE

The pupa is the stage between the larva and the adult in insects that undergo complete metamorphosis. Inside the pupa the larva's body is being remade into the adult. Most pupae do not feed. Some can wriggle if they are disturbed by a *predator*.

Stag beetle pupae survive the winter in rotting wood. They "hatch" into the adults in spring.

Many insect larvae form pupae in the soil, sometimes a few inches below the surface.

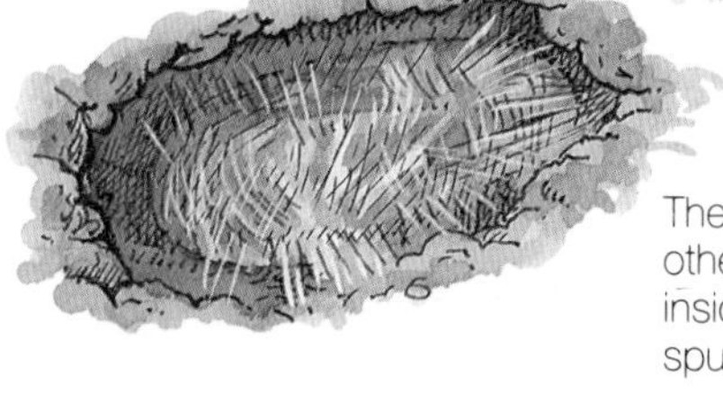

The pupae of **moths** and many other insects are often formed inside a *cocoon* of silk. The silk is spun by the larvae.

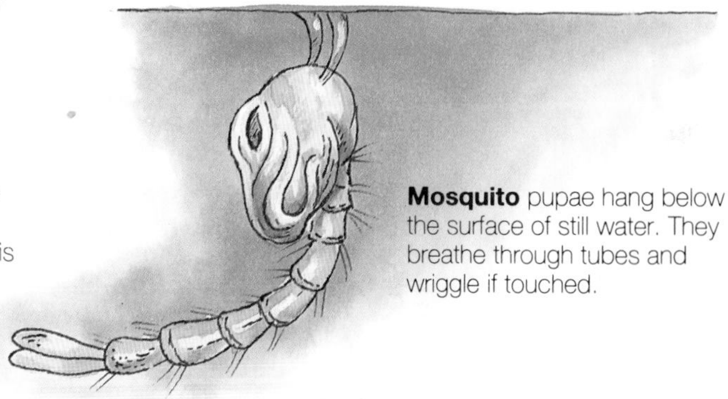

Mosquito pupae hang below the surface of still water. They breathe through tubes and wriggle if touched.

MOLTING AWAY

The young of some insects do not form a pupa but grow into adults through a series of growth stages. This is called incomplete metamorphosis. Grasshoppers, cockroaches, and termites all grow in this way. Their young are called *nymphs*. At each stage the nymph's tough, outer skin splits and the insect climbs out. This is called molting. At each molt the nymph gets larger. Eventually, the skin splits and out climbs the adult. It has wings and will grow no more. The **dragonfly** shown below molted many times and took two years to become an adult.

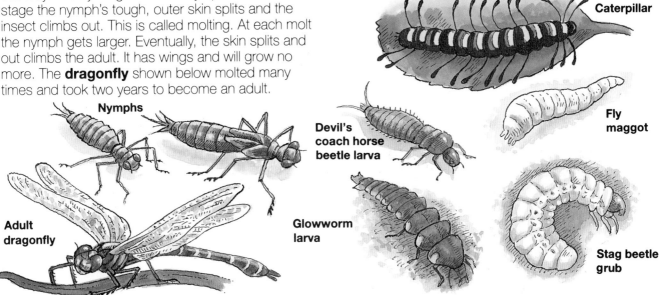

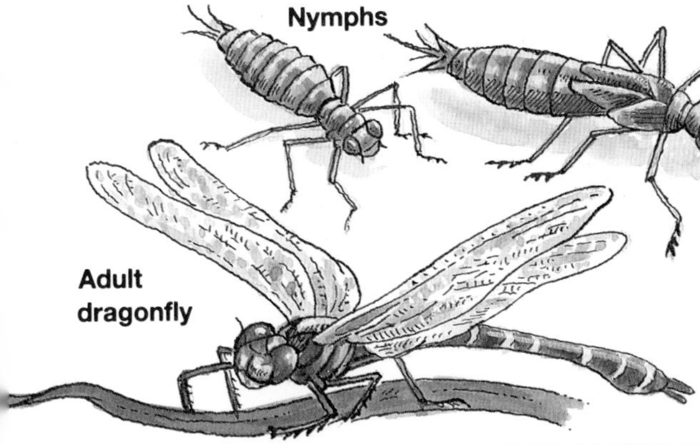

THE YOUNG ONES

The larvae of insects that undergo complete metamorphosis are often called by other names. Beetle larvae are often called grubs, while fly larvae are often called maggots. Here are some different kinds of larvae.

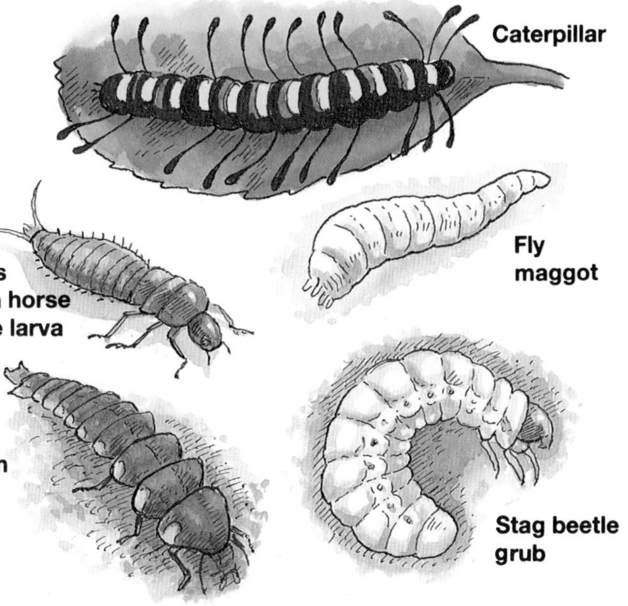

Happy families

Take a good look at the larvae and pupae shown here. **Can you match them to their adult forms?**

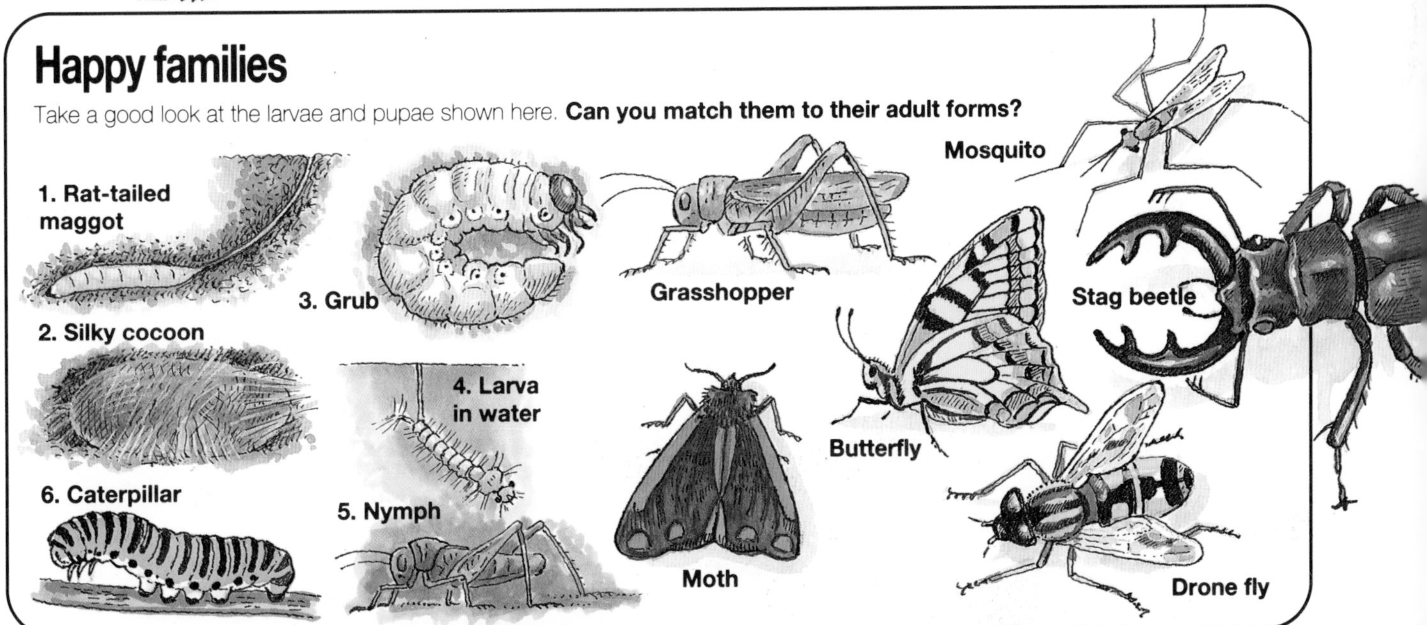

ANSWERS

HAPPY FAMILIES

1. The **rat-tailed maggot** is the larva of the **drone fly**.
2. The **silky cocoon** is that of the **cinnabar** moth.
3. This curled, white **grub** is that of a **stag beetle**.
4. Like their pupae, the **larvae** of **mosquitoes** hang upside-down in water.
5. **Grasshoppers** are insects that undergo incomplete metamorphosis. Their young are called **nymphs**.
6. This **caterpillar** is the larva of the **swallowtail butterfly**. Soon it will become a chrysalis, and later, an adult.

Moving

Insects move in many different ways. Their legs allow them to hop, walk, run, and swim. As well as legs, nearly all insects have wings. Many are expert fliers. Wings and legs enable insects to move to new places in search of food and to escape from animals that hunt and eat them.

Of course, legs and wings are not just used for moving about. Many insects use their legs for catching and gripping food. Wings are often used to attract mates by being brightly colored or patterned, by producing scent, or by making sounds.

Fleas are *parasites*. They live on the bodies of birds and mammals where they feed on blood. They have no wings. Instead, fleas have very large back legs which enable them to jump from one animal to another.

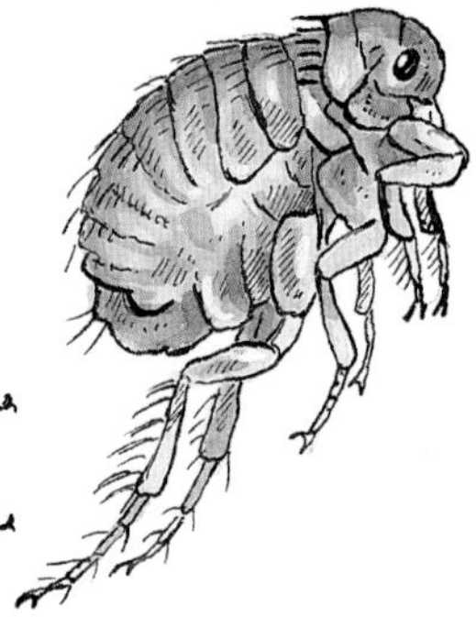

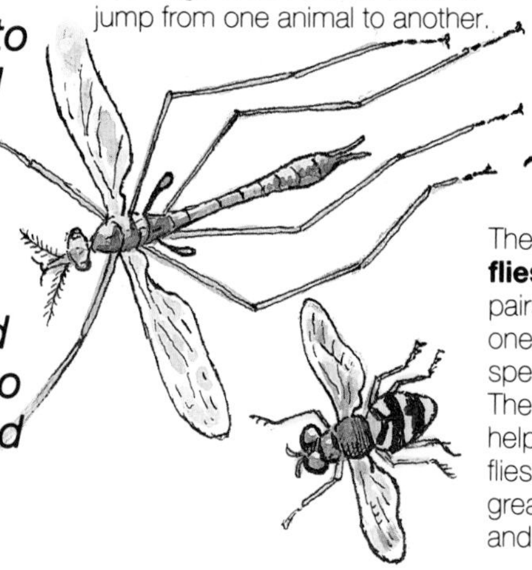

The best fliers of all are the true **flies**. Most insects have two pairs of wings, flies have only one. The back pair have become special structures called halteres. These give the fly balance and help it to control its flight. Most flies can fly very fast and with great agility. Some can hover and even fly backward.

On the move

These insects want to get to the other side of the pond as quickly as possible. **How do you think each one would travel?**

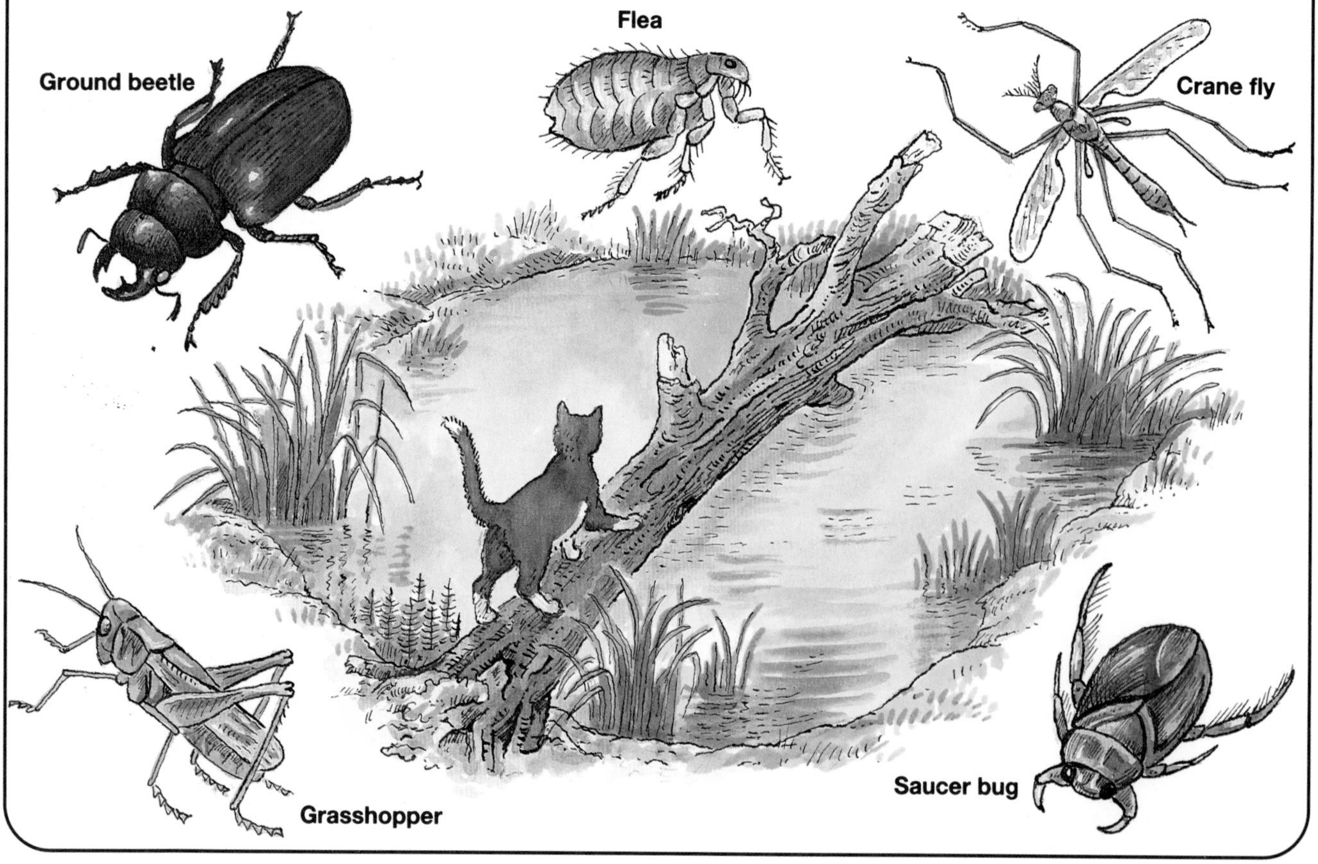

Beetles do not have a front pair of wings. Instead they have a pair of tough wing cases which, when closed, protect the body of the insect. As the beetle takes off, the wing cases spread wide and the back wings unfold.

In flight, the wing cases help to give the beetle lift. The back wings beat backward and forward to drive the beetle through the air.

The young of **butterflies** and **moths** are called **caterpillars**. The looper caterpillar, shown here, has the six legs that all insects have plus an extra two pairs of *claspers* at the end of its body. The caterpillar crawls by first pushing its front end forward. The front legs grip the twig, while the claspers are drawn up close behind them, so that the body forms a loop.

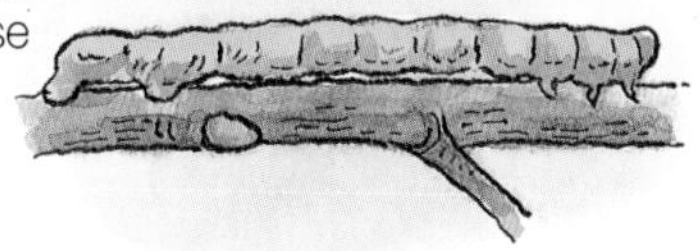

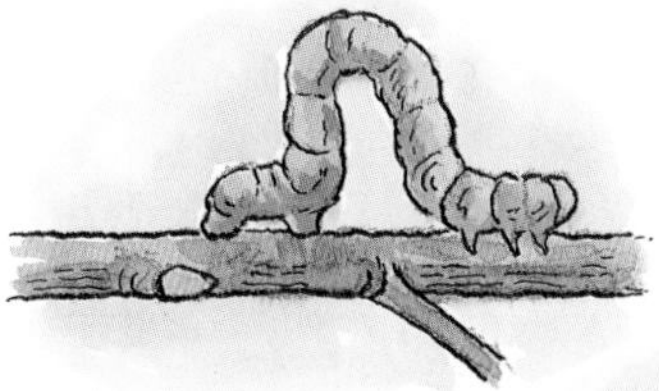

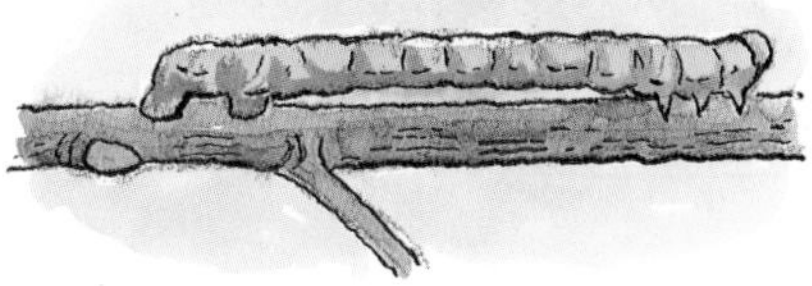

Divers and skaters

Several species of insects live on or in the water. They use their legs to swim or skate. Many can still fly from one pond to another if they need to.

Water boatmen have large back legs that propel them through the water like oars. They swim upside-down waiting to catch their *prey* in their shorter front legs.

Pond skaters do not actually get their feet wet. They walk on the surface of the water with their long thin legs.

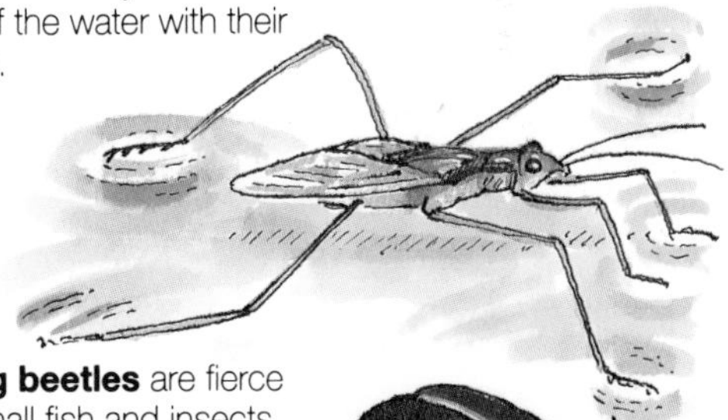

Great diving beetles are fierce hunters of small fish and insects. They store their air supply under their wings and have to keep swimming to avoid floating back to the surface.

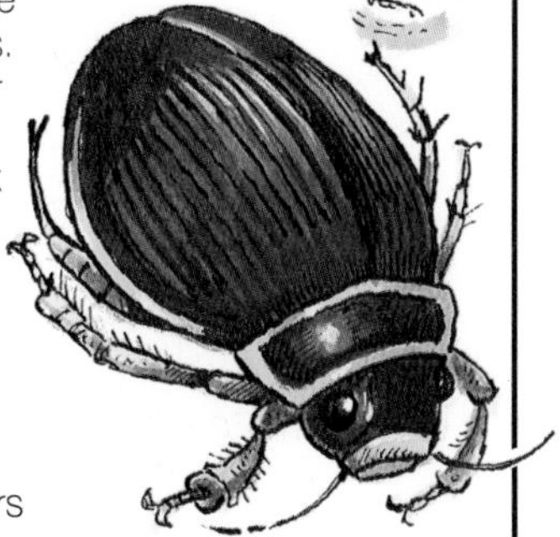

Whirligig beetles spin on the surface of the water. Their back legs are flat and fringed with hairs and act like paddles.

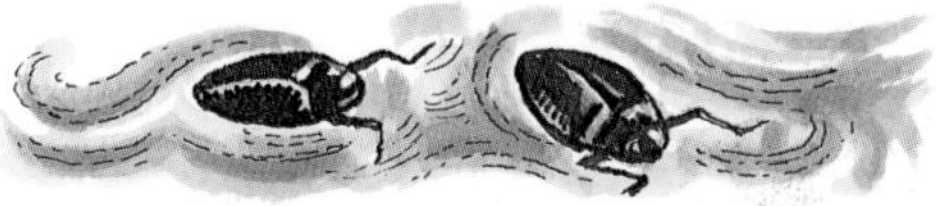

ANSWERS

ON THE MOVE

The **saucer bug** would swim across the pond using its back legs as paddles.

The **grasshopper** would use its legs and wings to get across. Grasshoppers launch themselves into the air with their powerful legs and then beat their wings to fly.

The **ground beetle** could walk along the tree or spread its wing cases and fly.

The **crane fly** would fly, using its halteres for balance.

The **flea** can use its large back legs to hop on to the cat and hitch a ride!

Making sense

*How good an insect's eyesight is depends on its lifestyle. Insects normally have two large compound eyes, which are very good at detecting movement. Many also have simple eyes which are only sensitive to changes in light. Insects that live in dark places can hardly see at all. They make sense of their world using their **antennae**. All insects have antennae. They come in many shapes and sizes and have many uses. Some insects use them to detect movements in the air, others use them to smell food or mates.*

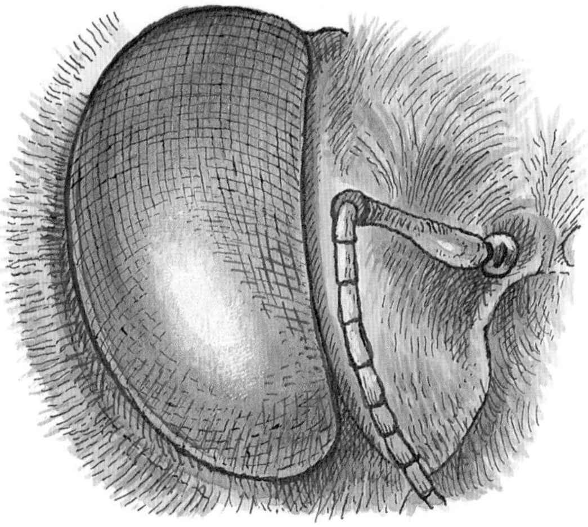

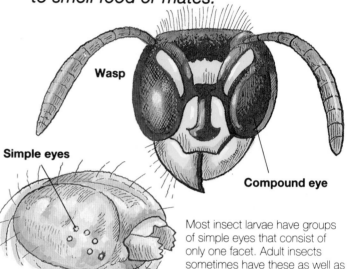

This is what a **bee's** compound eye looks like enlarged many times. The eye is made up of a large number of parts, or *facets*. Sight is important to flying insects. Scientists are not quite sure what insects see, but the more facets the eye has the sharper the picture will be and the easier it is to detect movement.

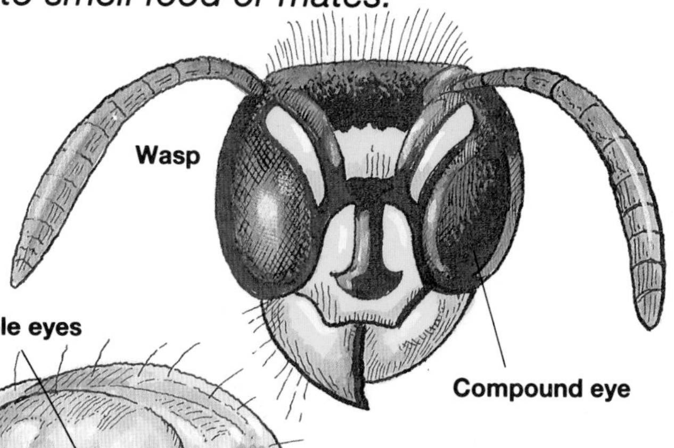

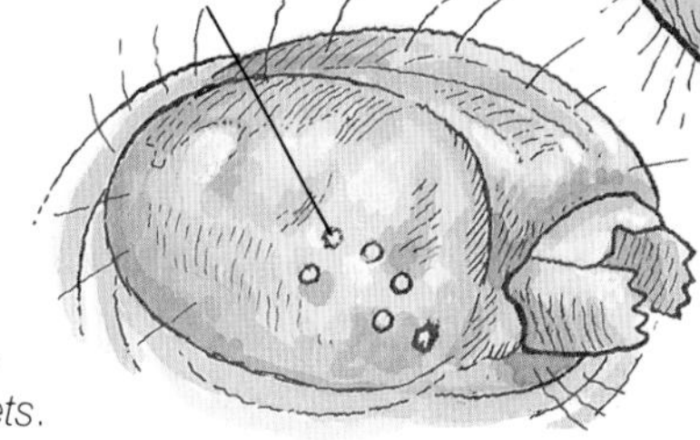

Most insect larvae have groups of simple eyes that consist of only one facet. Adult insects sometimes have these as well as compound eyes. Simple eyes can probably only detect changes in light and dark rather than movement.

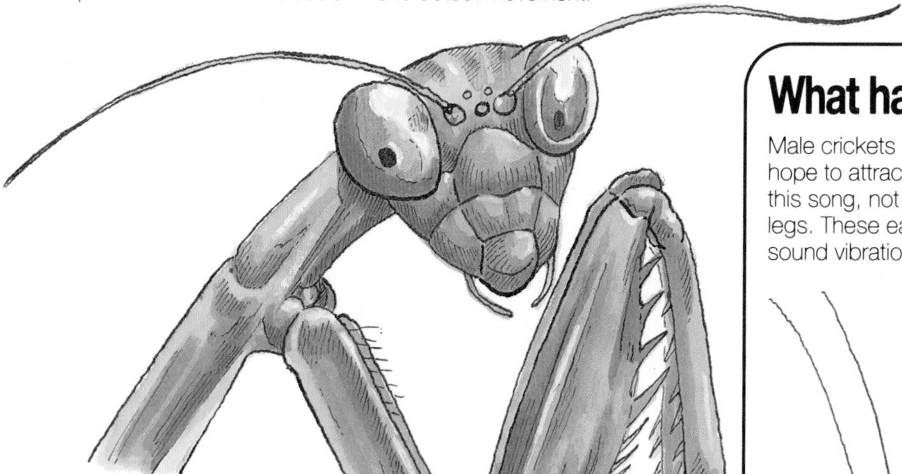

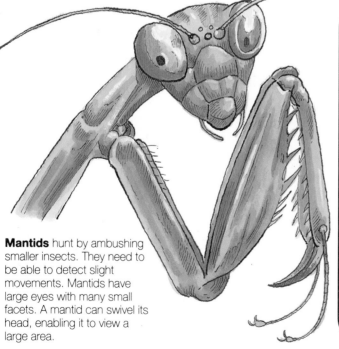

Mantids hunt by ambushing smaller insects. They need to be able to detect slight movements. Mantids have large eyes with many small facets. A mantid can swivel its head, enabling it to view a large area.

What have we ear?

Male crickets "sing" by rubbing their wings together. They hope to attract females with their song. The females can hear this song, not with ears on their heads, but with ears on their legs. These ears have a thin membrane which responds to sound vibrations.

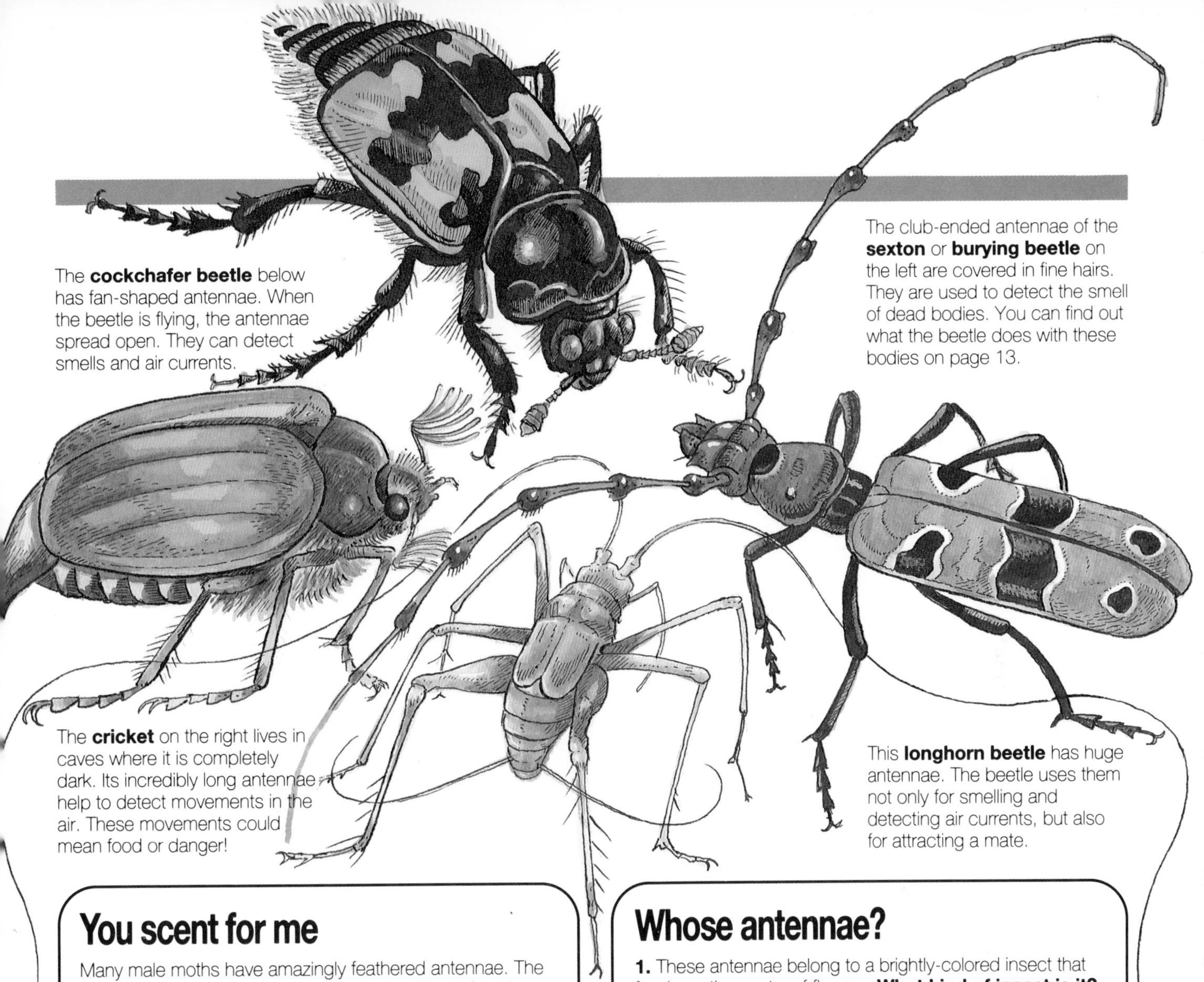

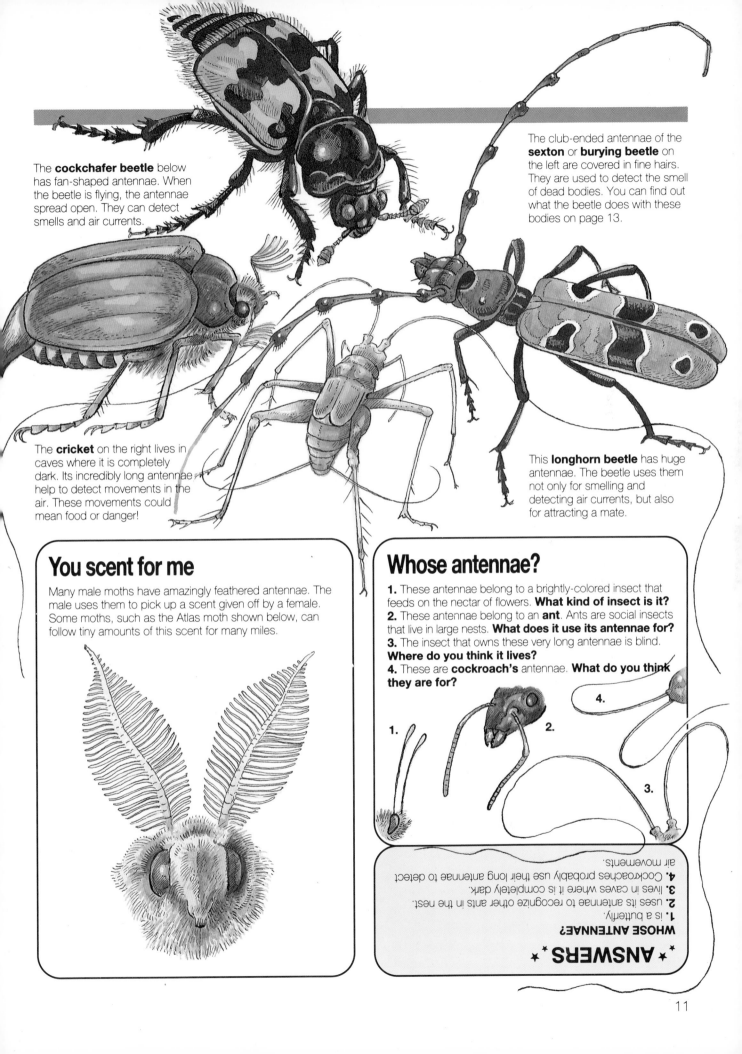

The **cockchafer beetle** below has fan-shaped antennae. When the beetle is flying, the antennae spread open. They can detect smells and air currents.

The club-ended antennae of the **sexton** or **burying beetle** on the left are covered in fine hairs. They are used to detect the smell of dead bodies. You can find out what the beetle does with these bodies on page 13.

The **cricket** on the right lives in caves where it is completely dark. Its incredibly long antennae help to detect movements in the air. These movements could mean food or danger!

This **longhorn beetle** has huge antennae. The beetle uses them not only for smelling and detecting air currents, but also for attracting a mate.

You scent for me

Many male moths have amazingly feathered antennae. The male uses them to pick up a scent given off by a female. Some moths, such as the Atlas moth shown below, can follow tiny amounts of this scent for many miles.

Whose antennae?

1. These antennae belong to a brightly-colored insect that feeds on the nectar of flowers. **What kind of insect is it?**
2. These antennae belong to an **ant**. Ants are social insects that live in large nests. **What does it use its antennae for?**
3. The insect that owns these very long antennae is blind. **Where do you think it lives?**
4. These are **cockroach's** antennae. **What do you think they are for?**

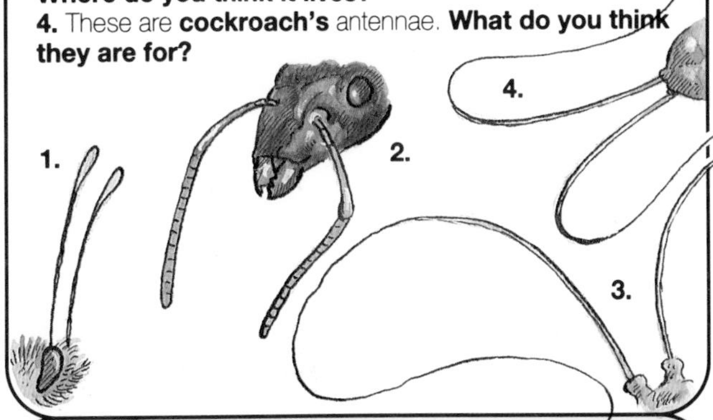

ANSWERS

WHOSE ANTENNAE?

1. is a butterfly.
2. uses its antennae to recognize other ants in the nest.
3. lives in caves where it is completely dark.
4. Cockroaches probably use their long antennae to detect air movements.

Eating out

Between them the different kinds of insects eat just about anything. The leaves and roots of every kind of plant, fungi, nectar, other insects, slugs, worms, snails, and dung are just a few things that appear on their menu. They also eat dead plants and animals, and natural products such as cloth and wax.

The kind of mouthparts an insect has depends on what it eats. It could have jaws for chewing, a tongue for licking, or a tube for sucking.

Most butterflies and moths do not have jaws. Instead they have a hollow tube called a *proboscis*. This **hawk moth** feeds on nectar by pushing its long proboscis deep into the heart of the flower. The proboscis is curled up under the moth's head when it is not in use.

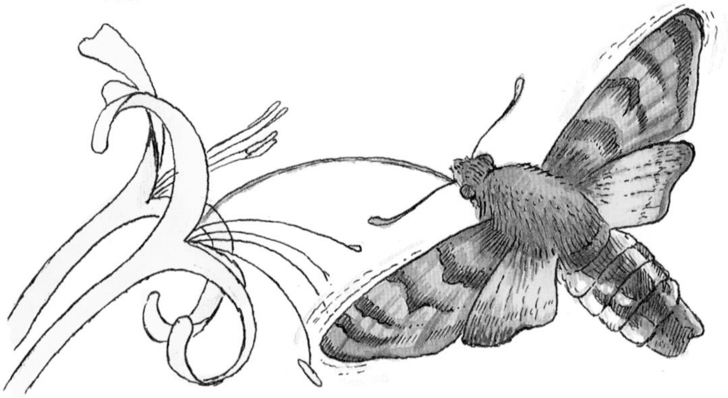

This **horsefly** feeds on the blood of other animals. It has long needle-like mouthparts for piercing the skin. Before sucking the blood, the horsefly injects its victim with a substance that prevents the blood from clotting. Plant bugs suck sap from plants using similar piercing mouthparts.

Grasshoppers and **crickets** eat tough plant material. Their mouthparts consist of a pair of sharp-edged jaws for cutting off pieces of plant. Behind the jaws are structures that hold and taste the food.

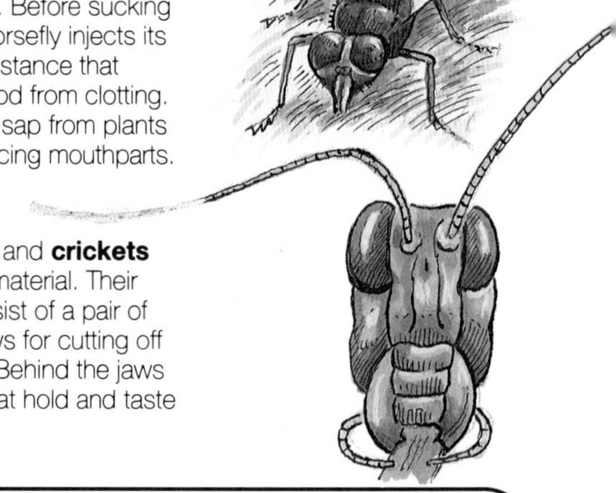

Hungry bugs

The insects on the left have not eaten for a long time. Take a close look at their mouthparts and any other clues you can see. **Can you match the insects to their food?**

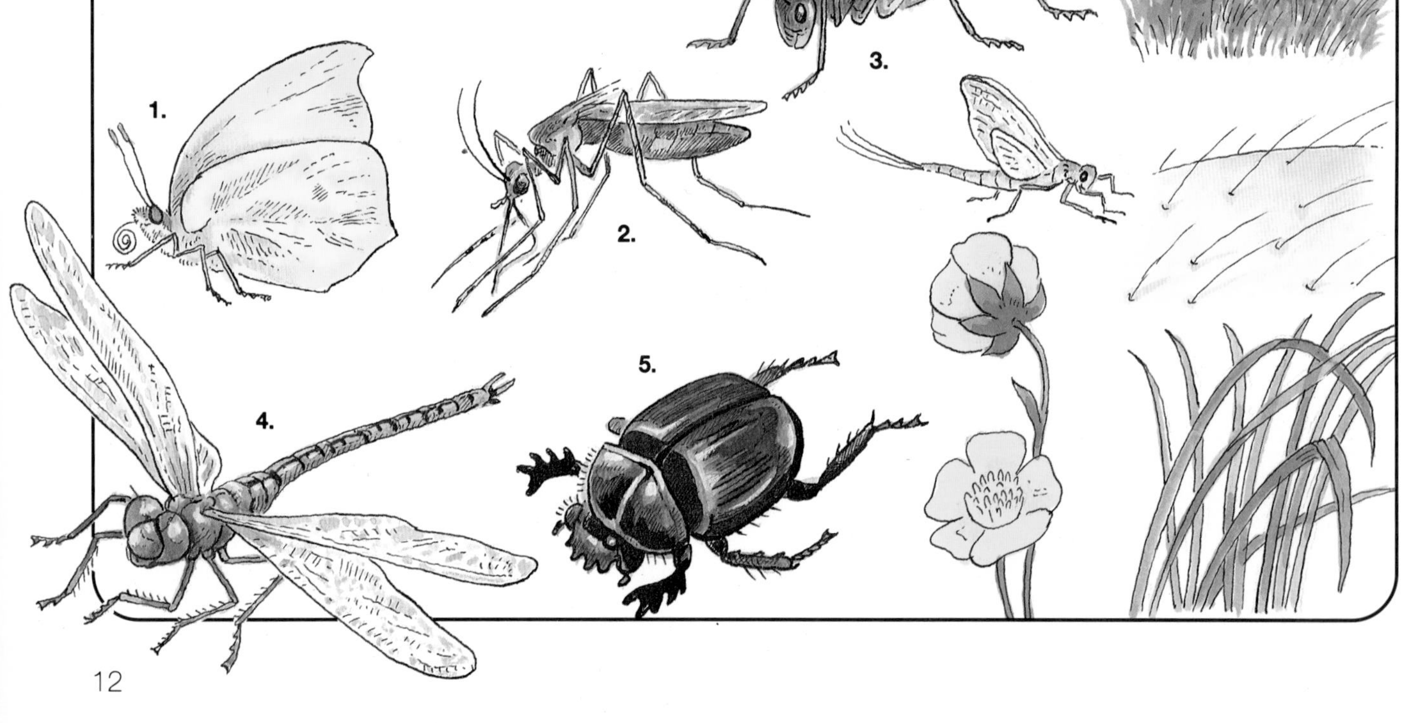

DIFFERENT FOODS

Insect larvae eat huge amounts of food because they are growing fast. Adult insects often eat only to give them energy to find mates and lay eggs. In some kinds of insects the adults and larvae live in different places on very different food.

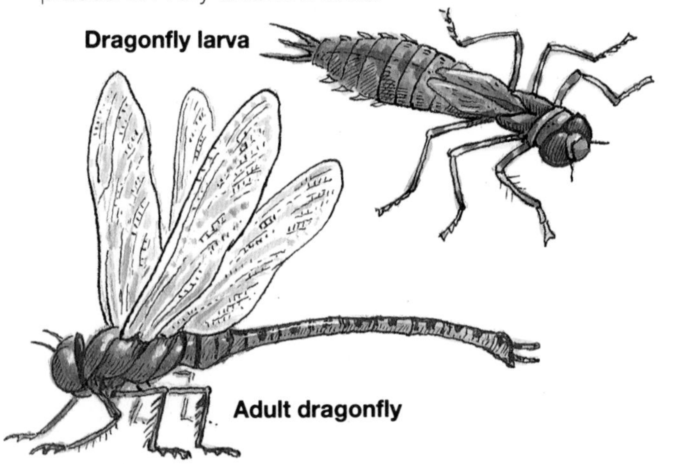

Dragonfly larvae live in the murky depths of ponds and lakes. They eat small creatures such as worms, tadpoles, and small fish. The adults live out of the water. They catch other insects as they fly and eat them with their powerful jaws.

Ant lions are the larvae of large, four-winged flies called Neuropterans. They dig funnel-shaped traps in sand and wait for ants and other insects to fall in. The victim slides down the funnel into the jaws of the ant lion. Its jaws pierce and suck up the juices of its prey. The adult eats other insects which it catches in flight.

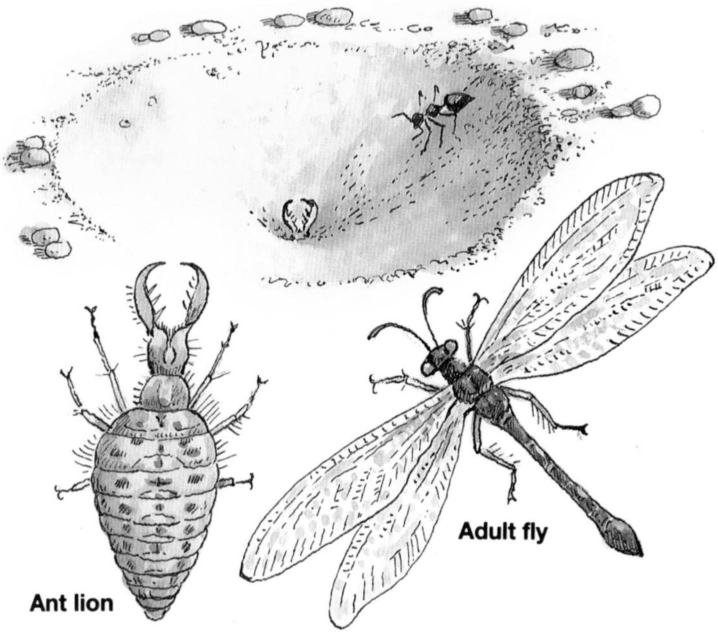

Buried treasure

Sexton or burying beetles use their sense of smell to find small dead animals such as mice. When the beetles have buried the mouse, the female lays her eggs nearby. The larvae then feed on the dead body.

Dung beetles, often named "tumble bugs,"care for their young by rolling a small piece of dung into a ball and burying it. The female lays an egg in the center of the ball. As the larva grows it eats the dung from inside. Later it emerges as an adult.

ANSWERS

HUNGRY BUGS

1. Butterflies uncoil their long proboscises to feed on the nectar of flowers.

2. This **mosquito** has piercing mouthparts for sucking the blood of mammals such as you and me.

3. Crickets have strong sharp-edged jaws for cutting the leaves of plants.

4. Dragonflies have strong, tooth-edged jaws for eating other insects. Dragonflies have also been known to swoop down and take small frogs and fish from ponds.

5. Dung beetles eat dung. They often eat more than their own weight in a day.

Staying alive

*Insects are food for many other animals. They are eaten by bats, birds, shrews, foxes, monkeys, other insects, and many others. With all these **predators** about, insects have had to develop many different ways of protecting themselves. One of the best ways is to blend in with their background by being **camouflaged**. Many insects have colors, patterns, and shapes which make them hard to see. Some are colored to look like leaves or the bark of trees. Others have blotches of color and strange shapes making them look like anything but insects. Some insects look so much like bits of plants that they are sometimes accidently eaten by plant-eating animals!*

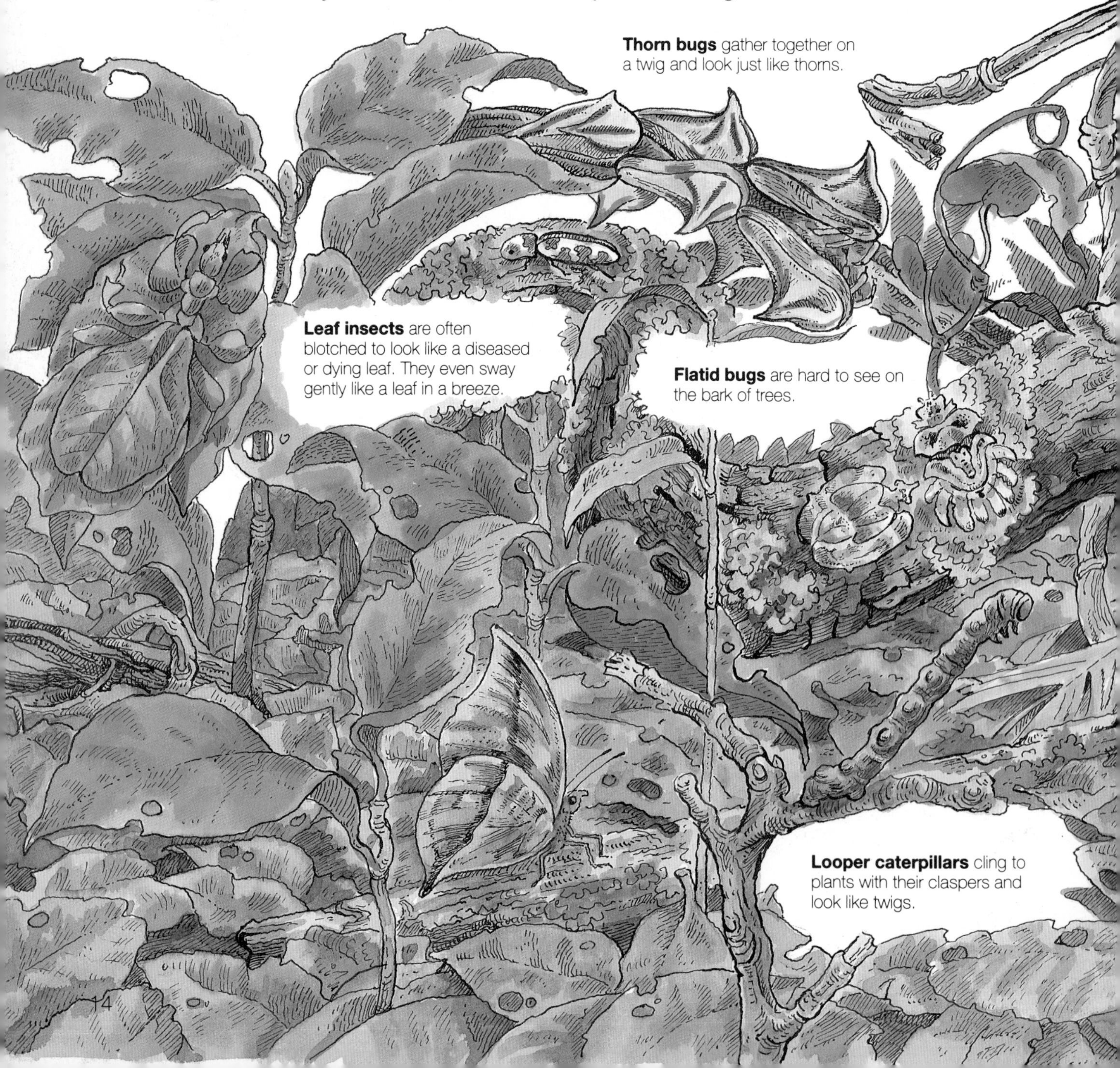

Thorn bugs gather together on a twig and look just like thorns.

Leaf insects are often blotched to look like a diseased or dying leaf. They even sway gently like a leaf in a breeze.

Flatid bugs are hard to see on the bark of trees.

Looper caterpillars cling to plants with their claspers and look like twigs.

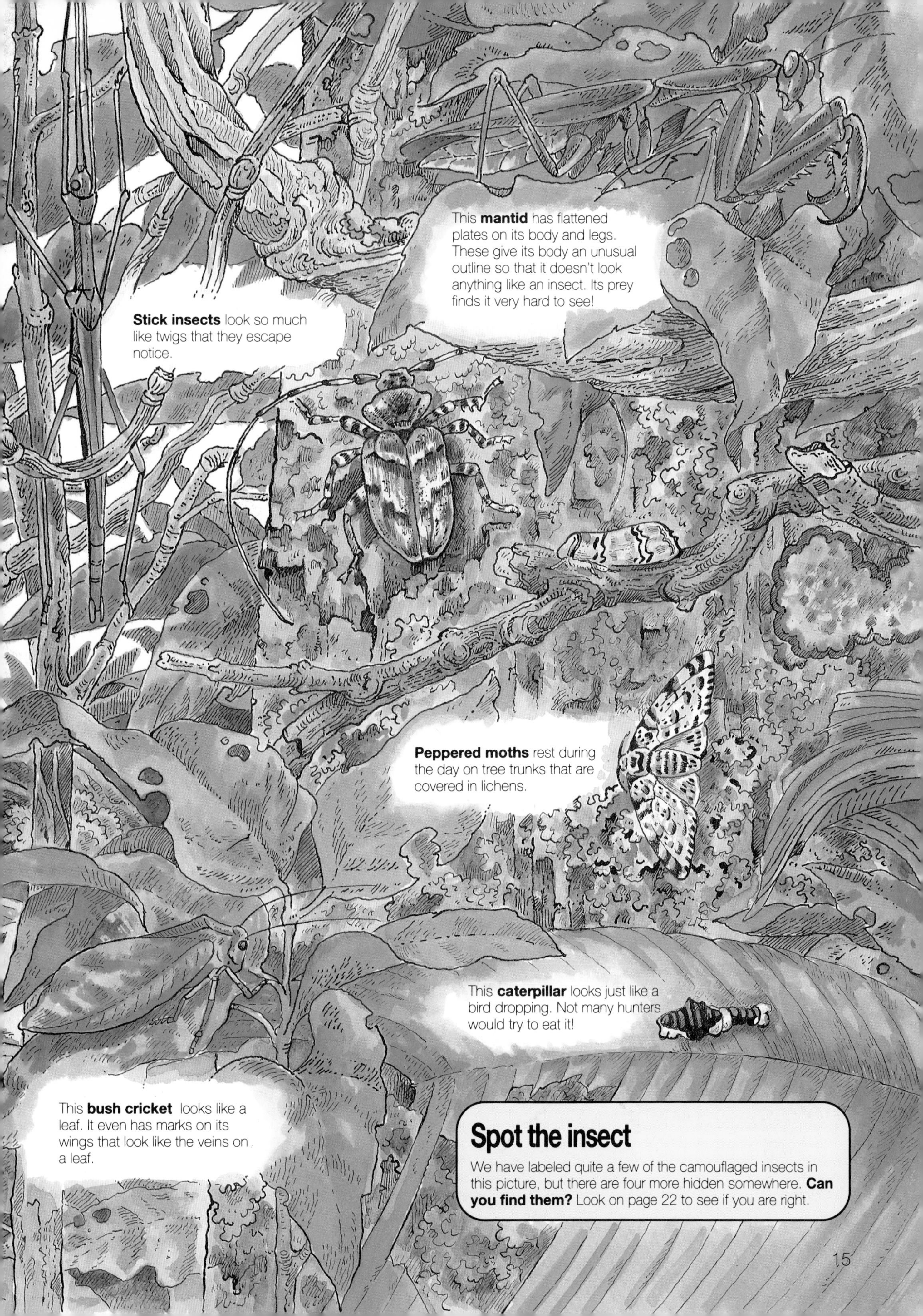

This **mantid** has flattened plates on its body and legs. These give its body an unusual outline so that it doesn't look anything like an insect. Its prey finds it very hard to see!

Stick insects look so much like twigs that they escape notice.

Peppered moths rest during the day on tree trunks that are covered in lichens.

This **caterpillar** looks just like a bird dropping. Not many hunters would try to eat it!

This **bush cricket** looks like a leaf. It even has marks on its wings that look like the veins on a leaf.

Spot the insect

We have labeled quite a few of the camouflaged insects in this picture, but there are four more hidden somewhere. **Can you find them?** Look on page 22 to see if you are right.

Hands off!

As you have seen, some insects avoid being eaten by blending in with their background. But there are other ways of staying alive. Some insects taste terrible and others have stings to defend themselves. These insects often have warning colors to show would-be predators that they should be avoided.

Others are protected by spines, flashing colors, jaws that bite hard, or the ability to make sudden noises. Perhaps the sneakiest way of staying alive is to pretend to be somebody else. Many harmless insects look just like, or ***mimic****, poisonous or stinging creatures and escape being eaten that way.*

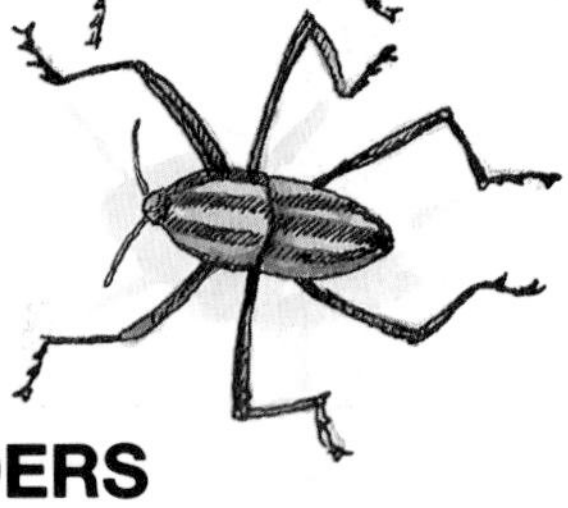

WARNING COLORS

Some insects, such as wasps and bees, are protected by stings. Others, like ladybugs and oil beetles, are poisonous. These insects usually advertize the fact that they are unpleasant to eat by being brightly colored. Warning colors are often red, black, and white, or black and yellow.

GREAT PRETENDERS

Many insects look and behave like other creatures. They are called mimics. Usually they are harmless insects pretending to be harmful. In the pictures above you can see a beetle that looks like an ant, a fly pretending to be a wasp, and a weevil that is mimicking a spider.

Not what you think

The insects shown here are protected from predators in one way or another. Look carefully at these two pages and the previous pages on camouflage. **Can you tell how these insects are protected from their enemies?**

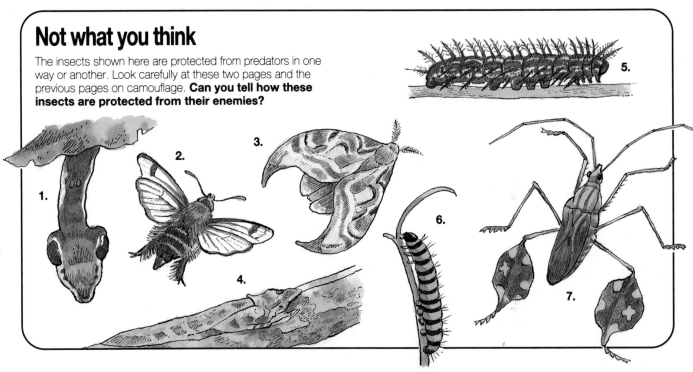

5.

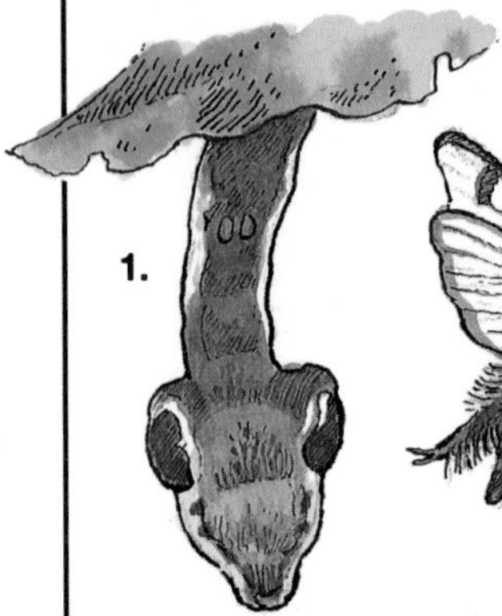

1.

2.

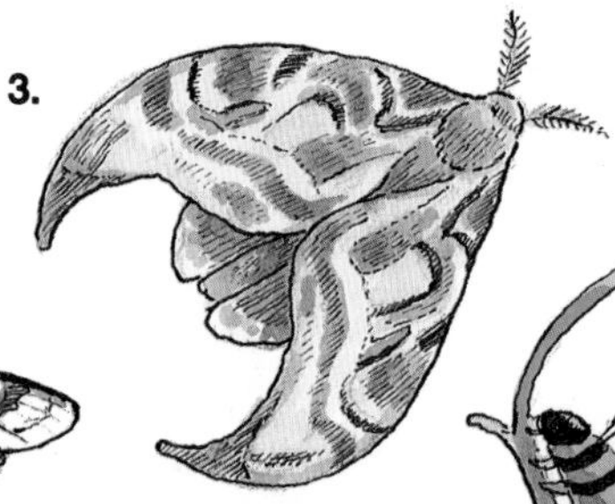

3.

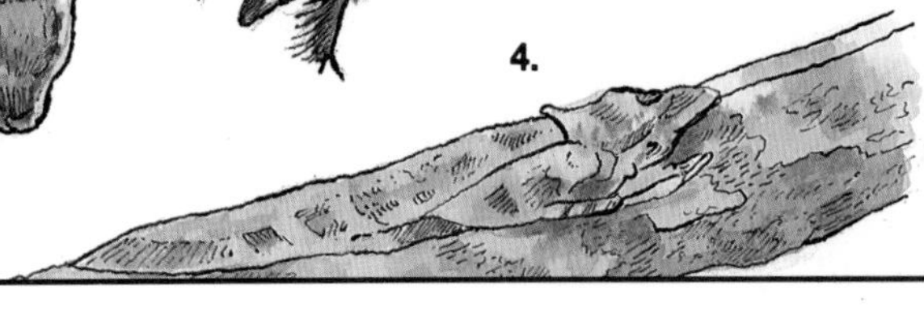

4.

6.

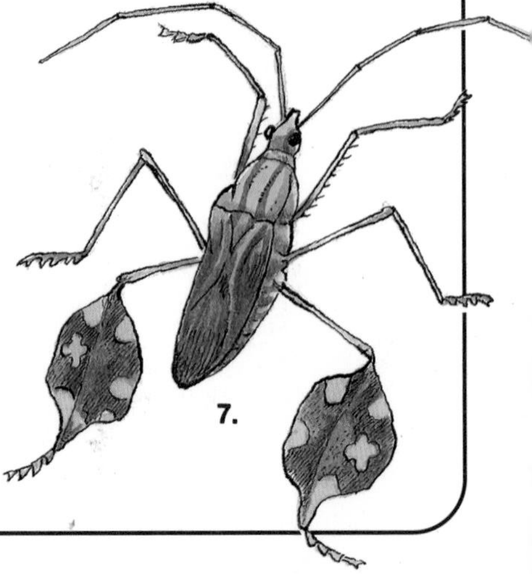

7.

SNAP, CRACKLE, AND POP!

Insects have developed an amazing number of ways to avoid being eaten. These include spines, noises, and even explosions.

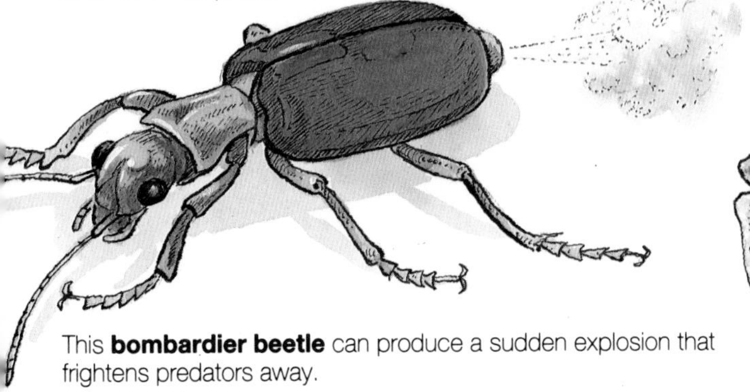

This **bombardier beetle** can produce a sudden explosion that frightens predators away.

The spines on the legs of this **cricket** can wound a would-be predator.

This **click beetle** has a spine on its thorax which fits into a notch on its abdomen, bending the body over. When the spine is released from the notch, its body is thrown into the air with a sudden click and startles the predator.

Shock tactics

Many insects hide the markings on their wings when they are resting. When they open their wings suddenly the flash of color is sometimes enough to startle a predator and give the insect time to escape.

Some insects avoid being eaten because they have markings on their wings that look like huge eyes. A predator may think that it has come across a much larger animal and leave the insect alone.

ANSWERS

NOT WHAT YOU THINK

1. Not only does this **hawk moth caterpillar** have eye markings, but its thorax is puffed up so that it looks like a snake's head.

2. This **moth** holds its furry legs against its body so that it looks like a hairy bee. Bees, of course, have stings!

3. When at rest with its wings folded, the **Atlas moth** looks just like a dead leaf.

4. This **bush cricket** from India looks just like a piece of bark and cannot be seen.

5. Birds probably avoid this **caterpillar** because its spines are unpleasant to touch and horrible to swallow.

6. This **cinnabar moth** caterpillar, which is poisonous, has warning colors of black and orange stripes.

7. This **bug** waves the "flags" on the end of its legs to distract predators from attacking its body.

Team work

Social insects are insects that live and work together as a team. This team is in fact one family because all the insects have the same mother. She is the queen of the colony. Ants, termites, and some wasps and bees are all social insects. Within their nests these insects have a well-organized system. Each insect has its own job to perform.

Termites form the biggest insect colonies. Some build nests underground or inside tree trunks, but the most fascinating are the termite mounds of Africa and Australia. The mounds can be up to 20 feet tall and contain as many as five million termites.

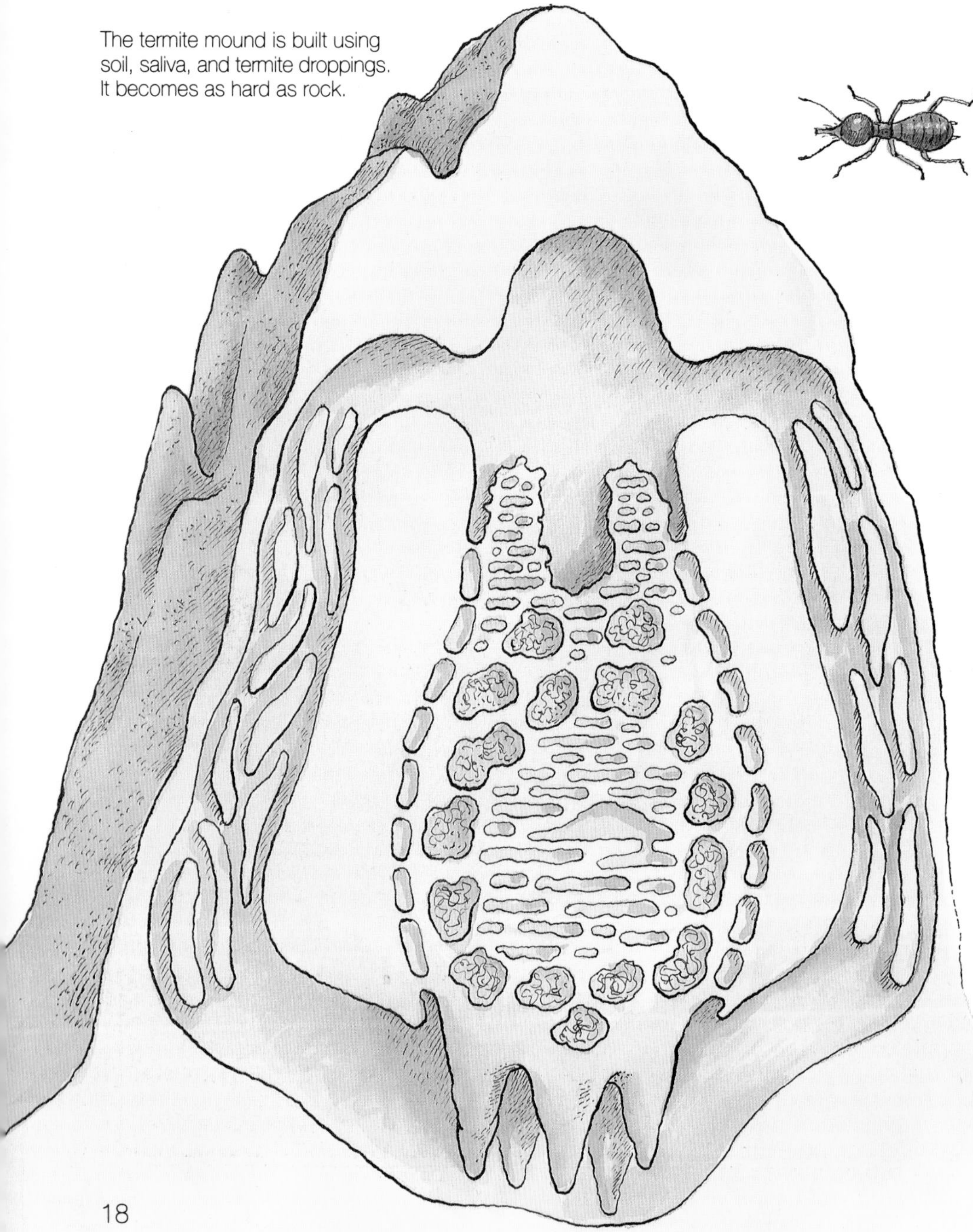

The termite mound is built using soil, saliva, and termite droppings. It becomes as hard as rock.

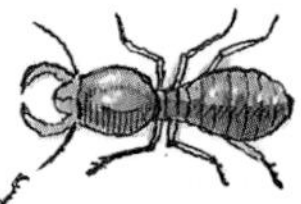

Soldier termites have large heads. They use them to block the entrances when the nest is attacked. Some have strong jaws for defense, while others have a snout from which they can squirt a sticky fluid onto the enemy.

Workers leave the nest and forage for food under the protection of the soldiers. They also look after the nest, feed the king and queen, and tend the young.

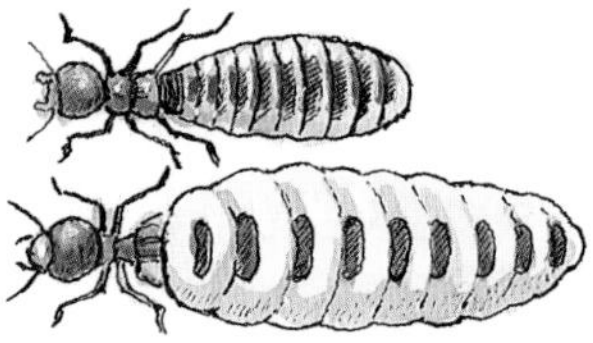

Each nest has a **king** and **queen**. The queen's abdomen becomes swollen with eggs and she is unable to move. She can lay up to 30,000 eggs each day.

Air flows through the tunnels keeping the temperature in the mound just right, even if it's very hot outside.

Some termites grow a special fungus to eat. Others feed on wood, leaves, and soil.

Termites need water and a damp atmosphere. Deep shafts lead down to the moist earth. Workers carry water droplets up to the main nest.

BUMBLE BEES

Bumble bees are social insects. They use their long tongues to get nectar from flowers. The nectar is stored in a special "honey stomach" to be used later in the nest.

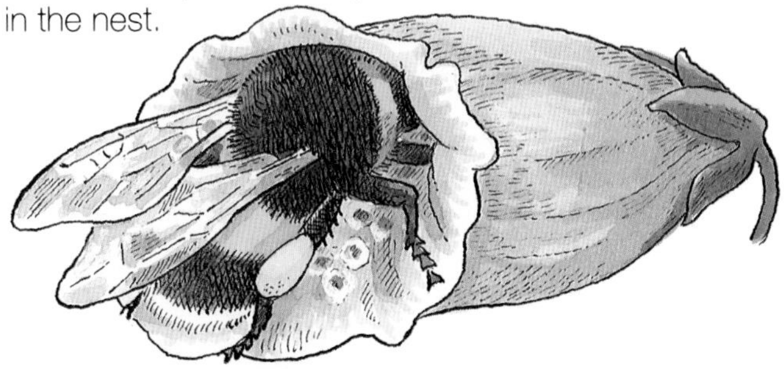

DANCING BEES

Honeybees perform "waggle" dances to tell the other bees in the hive where they can find food. The dance is done in a "figure of eight" pattern. It tells the bees which direction to fly and how far to go.

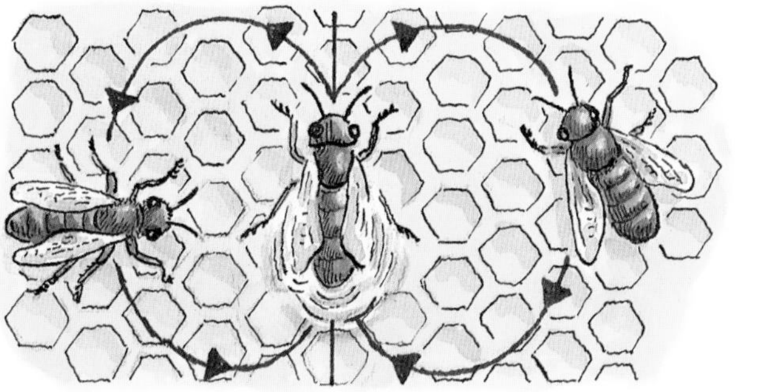

IN THE HIVE

A bee hive has only one queen, a few hundred males, and up to 60,000 sterile (non egg-laying) females called workers. The honeycomb is made of wax which the females produce from glands in their abdomens. The queen lays an egg in each cell which hatches into a larva after three days. The rest of the comb is filled with honey which the workers feed to the larvae.

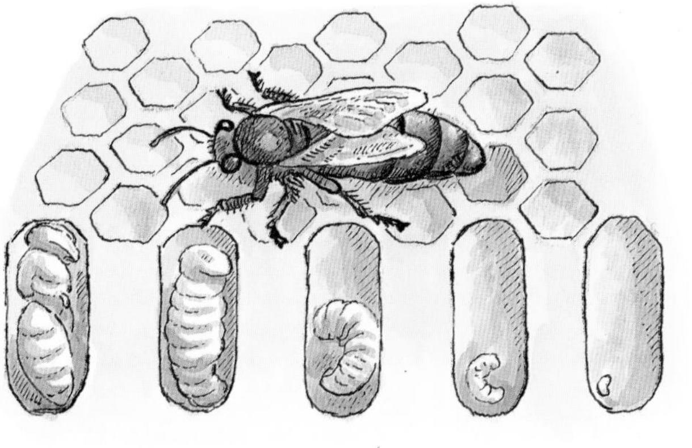

All sown up

Weaver ants line up along the edge of a leaf and reach up to grab hold of another leaf. Other workers move back and forth binding the edges of the leaves together with a sticky silk thread. The silk is produced by live ant larvae which the workers carry in their jaws. The resulting nest is a hollow ball of leaves.

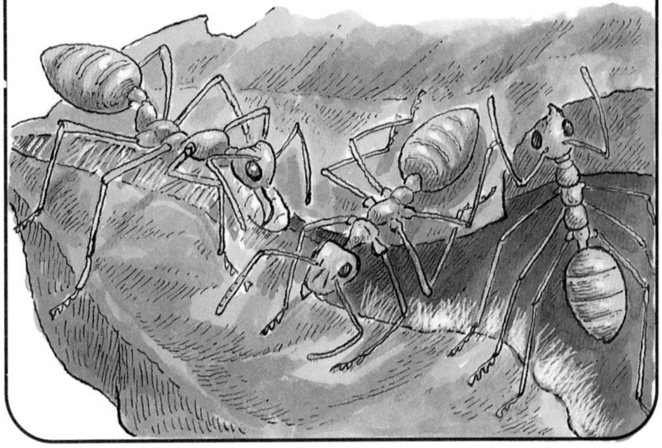

Strange ants

These **ants** hang upside-down in the nest and do not move. Their abdomens are swollen with water and nectar that the other ants have fed to them. **What do you think they are for?**

ANSWERS

STRANGE ANTS

These strange ants are called **honeypot ants**. During the dry season in desert areas there are no flowers for the ants to feed from. Honeypot ants are kept as food containers to keep the rest of the colony alive during this time.

Good, bad, and ugly

Many people only see insects as a nuisance, which in many cases is true. Plant-eating insects can destroy valuable food crops. Others spread diseases and give us irritating bites and stings. Even the most harmless insects are disliked because of their "creepy-crawlie" appearance.

Insects are, however, vital for life on earth. They pollinate plants, help to remove dung and dead bodies, and they are food for animals and humans.

Fleas are parasites which means that they live and feed on living animals. They cling to the animals' fur and suck their blood. As well as causing discomfort, they can also spread diseases.

Colorado beetles destroy potato crops. They move from plant to plant, killing them by eating the leaves and buds.

Mosquitos pierce the skin and suck blood. As they go from one person to another, they spread diseases such as malaria and yellow fever. These diseases can kill people.

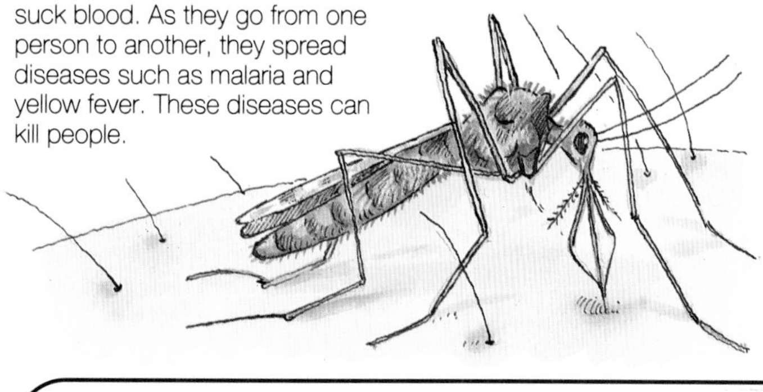

Deathwatch beetles eat wood. They bore tunnels through wooden beams and can seriously weaken buildings.

Big eaters

Occasionally locusts gather in large numbers and move in a swarm. A swarm can consist of a thousand million locusts. They have been known to eat 20,000 tons of green plants in a single day. These plants may be crops planted by people. Locust swarms can now be detected by satellite and destroyed before they can do great harm.

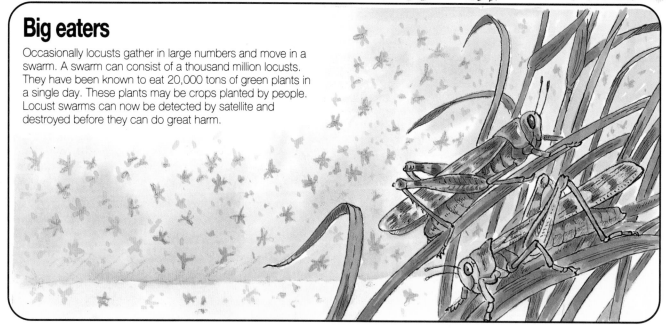

Many animals depend on insects for food. The **anteater** pushes its long snout into an ants' nest and laps up the ants with its long, sticky tongue.

Some people also eat insects. The plump and juicy larvae, called **wichetty grubs**, of some kinds of moth are very tasty. **Honeypot ants** make a sweet snack, while some **green ants** have a lime flavor.

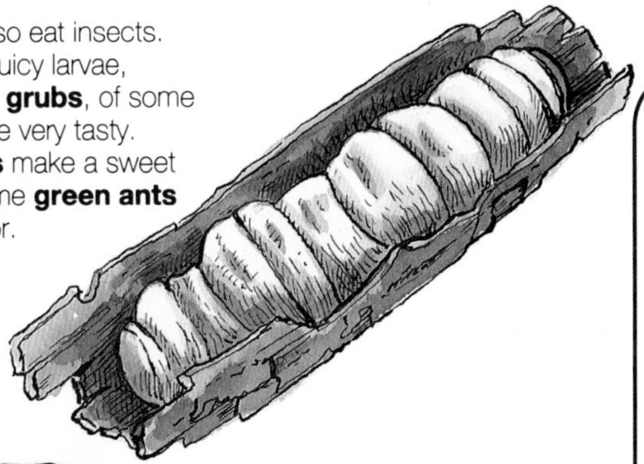

Some insects are good at removing waste. The larvae of the **yellow dung fly** feed on cow dung. This breaks down the dung so that it nourishes the soil and helps plants to grow.

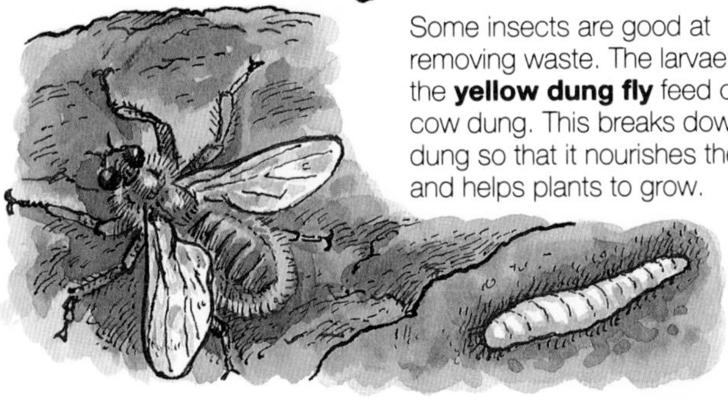

Insects can be used to control crop-eating pests. This is safer than using chemicals. **Ladybugs** eat the **aphids** that would otherwise destroy plants.

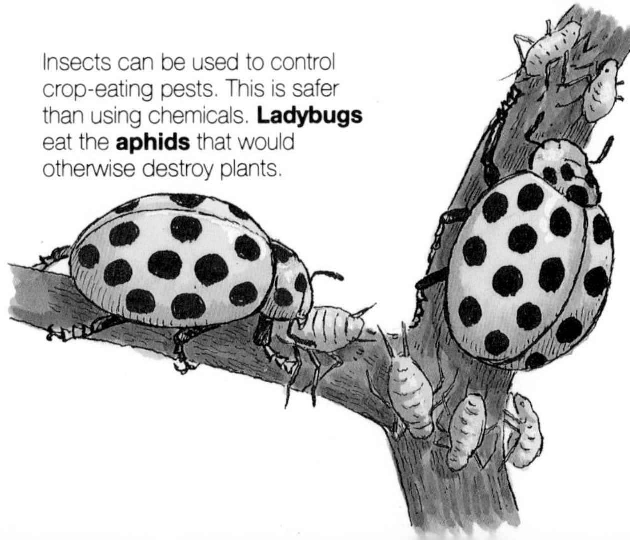

Plants need insects

Bees, flies, and butterflies help to pollinate crops and flowers. *Pollen* collects on the hairs that cover their bodies when they drink nectar from a flower. By carrying the pollen from one flower to another, the insect *pollinates* them. If this didn't happen, many plants would not be able to produce the seeds that grow into new plants.

Know your bugs

How well do you know your bugs? Here are a few questions about useful insects to test your knowledge.

1. These **maggots** are the young of **bluebottle flies**. **What do you think they eat, and why is this a good thing?**

2. Fireflies like this one glow in the dark to attract a mate. **How could this be useful to people?**

3. These caterpillars make long strands of silk when they are forming their cocoons. **How is this useful to people?**

4. Bees collect nectar and pollen from flowers. **What substance do they produce, and why is it useful to people?**

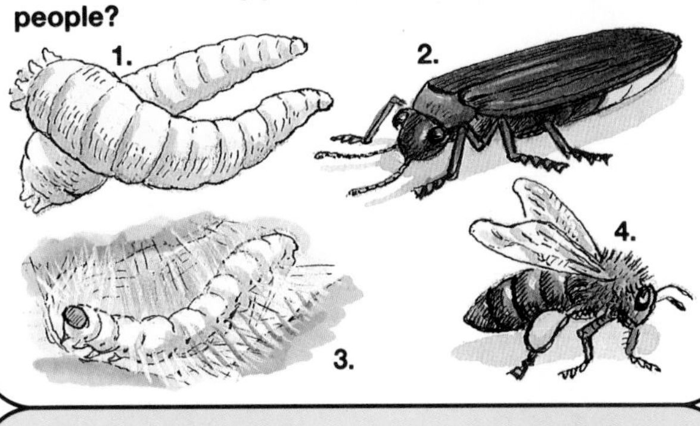

ANSWERS

KNOW YOUR BUGS

1. These **bluebottle maggots** live on the flesh of dead bodies. Without them, bodies would take a long time to decay.

2. In some countries people use **fireflies** to light their rooms!

3. Silk is a highly-valued material used to make fine clothes.

4. The substance is honey and we use it in our food. **Bees** also make wax which we use for polishing wood.

Quiz time

ALL IN ORDER

The pictures below show stages in the development of an insect that undergoes complete metamorphosis. Unfortunately, they are all in the wrong order. **Can you put them in order?**

Female beetle lays eggs

Eggs hatch

Adult emerging

Pupa

Newly emerged adult

Larva feeding

NEW DESIGNS

Imagine that you have been asked to design a new range of insects. **What colors should you make them?** Trace the drawings below onto another piece of paper. Then color them in following the instructions given with each one.

1. This **beetle** is poisonous. **What colors could it be?**

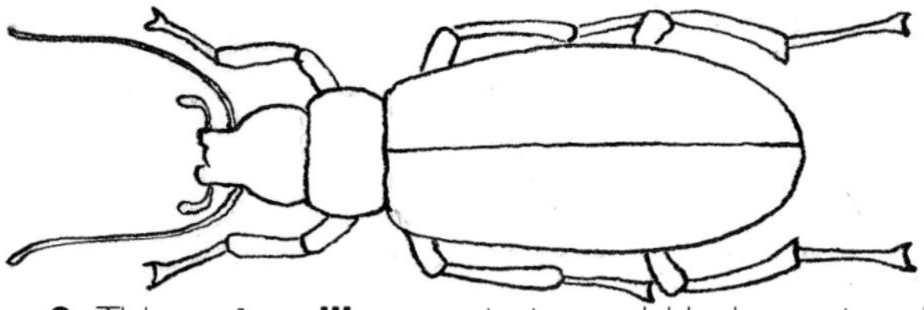

2. This **caterpillar** wants to avoid being eaten. **How should it look?**

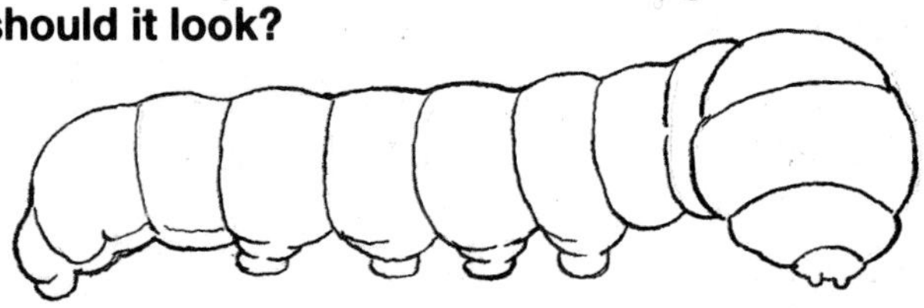

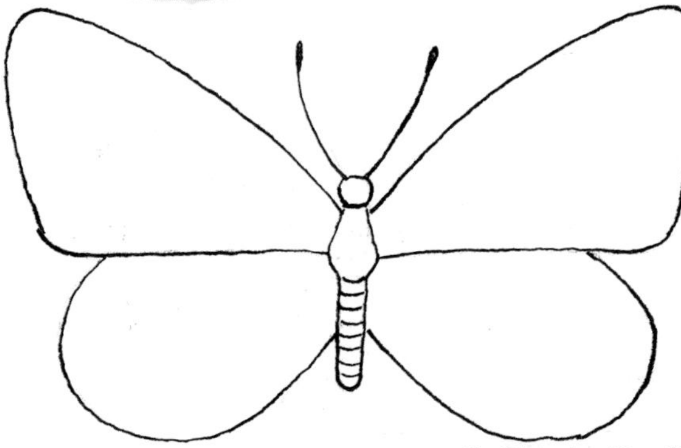

3. This **butterfly** should have markings which will scare off predators.

4. This harmless **fly** is mimicking an insect that has a sting. **What colors should it be?**

ANSWERS

ALL IN ORDER

The life cycle you have rearranged is that of a **beetle**. The correct order should be:

1. Female beetle lays eggs.
2. Eggs hatch
3. Larva feeding
4. Pupa
5. Adult emerging
6. Newly emerged adult flying away

NEW DESIGNS

1. This **butterfly** should have eye markings to scare predators as shown on page 17.

2. The **beetle** should be colored with spots or stripes of red, black, and white or black and yellow.

3. The most obvious insect for the **fly** to mimic is a **wasp**. It should be striped with black and yellow.

4. The **caterpillar** could be colored with black and yellow stripes, with eye spots, or it could look like a bird's dropping as shown on page 15.

STAYING ALIVE

In the illustration of camouflaged insects on pages 14 and 15 there is a **kalima butterfly** below the leaf insect and to the left of the looper caterpillar. There is a **lichen longhorn beetle** lurking below right of the stick insect. To the right of this longhorn beetle is a **buff tip moth**. Finally, there is a **click beetle** below the thorn bugs.